Ricky Roogle

The pointless book

Absurd jokes and puzzles

AF176417

A short history of this book.

Bibliographic information of the German National Library:
The German National Library lists this publication in the
German National Bibliography; detailed bibliographic data are
available on the Internet at http://dnb.dnb.de.

© 2022 Ricky Roogle;1st edition
Cover art, text & illustrations © 2022 Ricky Roogle
Author contact: ricky.roogle@t-online.de
Herstellung und Verlag: BoD – Books on Demand,
Norderstedt
ISBN: 9783756224166

Wie ist das?

FSC
www.fsc.org
MIX
Papier aus ver-
antwortungsvollen
Quellen
Paper from
responsible sources
FSC® C105338

Broken mirror

The element of astonishment!

127

Oh!

330

A pack of sinks
pursued by stoppers.

The pointless riddle

Frodo invites seven of his dwarf friends to a garden party at his house. He has picked seven splendid apples and the seven dwarves are to divide the apples so that each gets an apple. However, one apple should remain in the apple basket. How can this be done?

Solution: A dwarf gets his apple in an apple basket.

Time Traveler:
"...and in future, we will all be ruled by these deadly androids.
What machines do you use in your time?"

Me:
"Well, I drive a Tesla, for example."

Time Traveler:

The primal pixel

Task for A-Levels

Find the error:

$$E = mc^2$$

Aliens that do senseless things

On a planet, far, far away, an alien being stands on a giant high bridge and says, "Twenty-one, twenty-one, twenty-one...". Comes another alien being by and asks, "What are you doing here?"

Then the first alien being suddenly pushes him off the bridge and says, "Twenty-two, twenty-two, twenty-two..."

Save the sheep

Entrance

Place with hidden message
(please rub away color to read)

But when he turns around, they fall over in shock.

The natives are hunting a giant forest bird.

What is that?

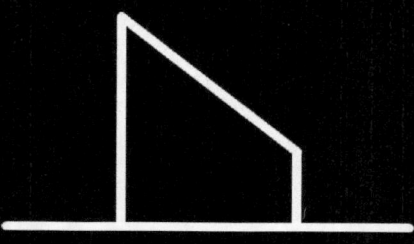

Titanic sinking

The useless puzzle

A man goes to a cemetery and stops in front of a grave. On the gravestone is his name, date of birth and date of death.

How is that possible?

Solution: The man is a gangster and is wanted and pursued worldwide. To mislead his pursuers, he has faked his death. Thus, the pursuers think he is dead and do not pursue him further.

The suspense of a good book...

The suspense of this book...

Trapped in the gully manhole

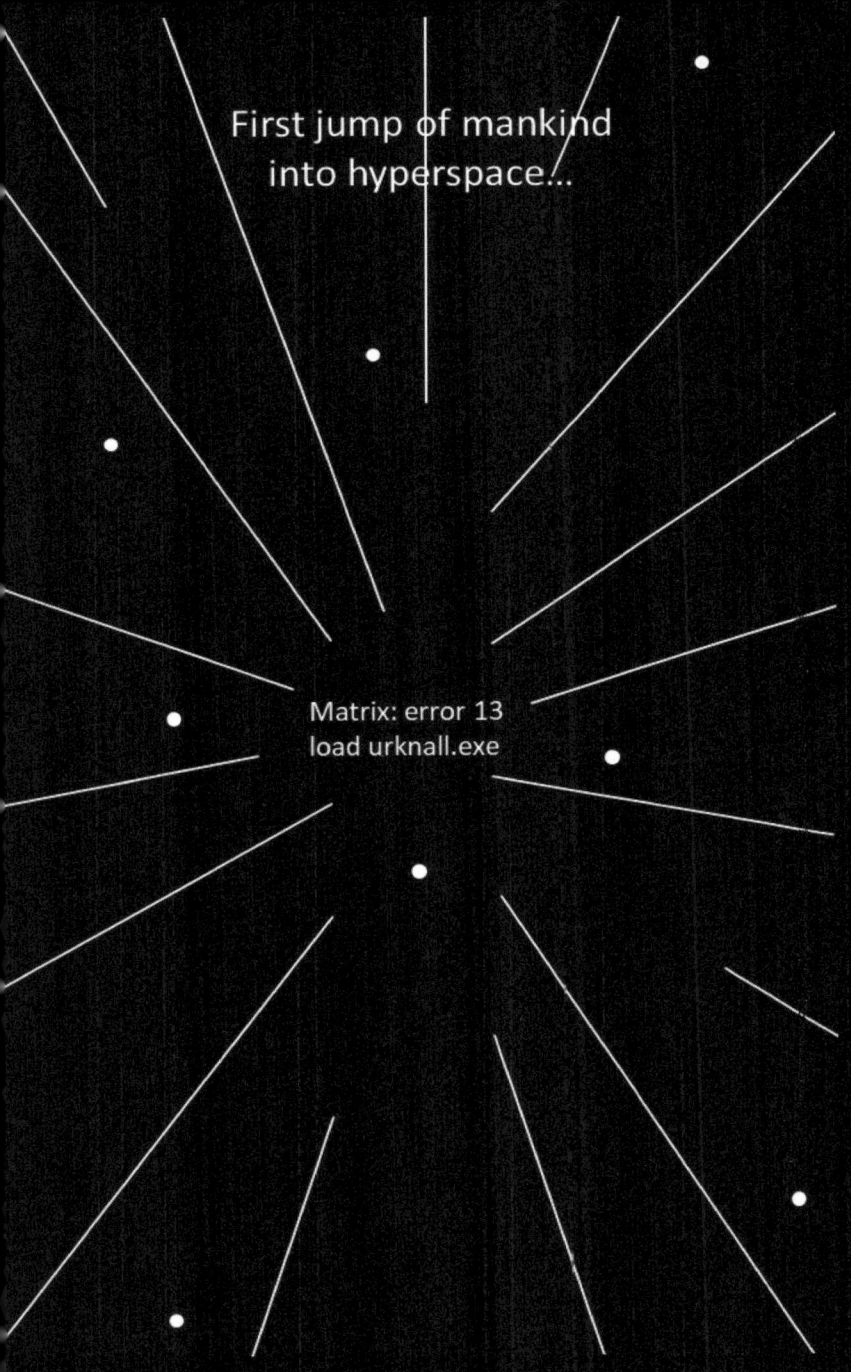

The riddle that no one needs

You are happy because your chicken breeding pays off. Every morning, you come out of the barn with a small basket full of freshly laid eggs. Now, the eggs have to be cooked before you can eat them. It takes you four minutes to boil four eggs. How long does it take you to boil ten eggs?

Solution: Of course once again, 4 minutes!

Mona Lisa's painting from behind

What is that?

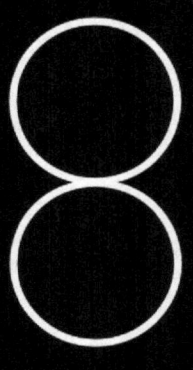

Two times four

Dave talked to his hand until it gave up.

You have 1 new message

Please press button to play

Black colour sample

Please ignore the hair on the pattern

Zebra behind bars

The worst puzzle in the world

Imagine that you have died and gone to heaven. There, you greet Eve and Adam by their names. Both are puzzled and ask:

"How did you know we were Adam and Eve?"

How could you have known?

Solution: Very simple, Adam and Eve are the only ones in heaven without a belly button!

A note suffering from giant growth.

One fine day the world famous cowmedian returned to her place of birth...

Why did the picture drop on the floor?

It did not know the framework conditions.

"You have just been flashedthinged."

The other day at the Emperor's School

"Anakin, for the last time, raise your visor to see!"

"Yes, master."

"Good afternoon. This is your captain speaking, I'm doing home office today."

"Finally, I see light at the end of the tunnel..."

To be continued →

What is that?

Star Wars

Recently, at the dentist

You need a crown.

Finally, someone who understands me.

Find the spot

Could not go shopping.

Bang! Extinct!

Meow Meow! Meow Meow! Answers the neighbor's cat.

Ruff Ruff! Ruff Ruff! Why is Bello so excited?

The black hole from front

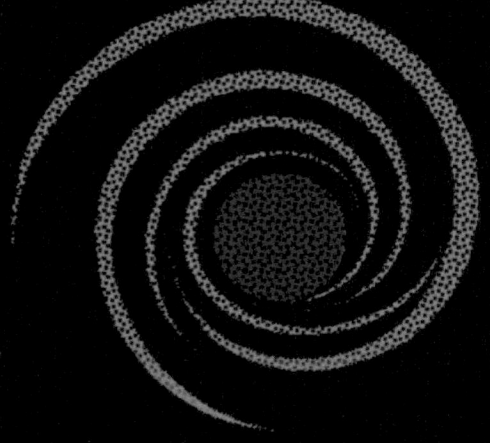

The black hole from behind

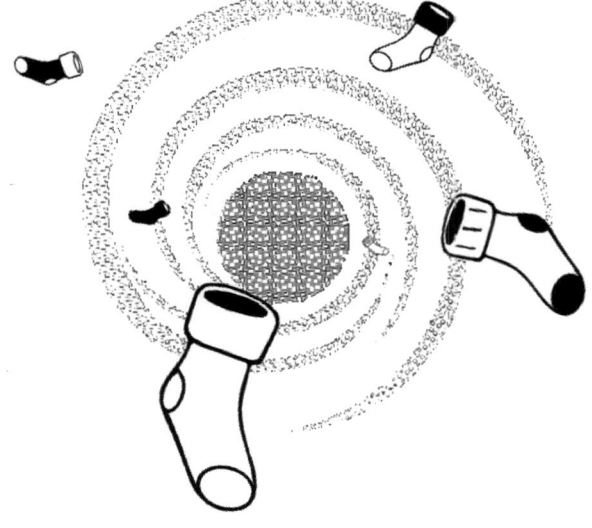

Dr. Jekell and Mr. Hyde

- the true story -

Unfortunately Dr. Jekell, as Mr. Hyde, could not remember the reversion potion and thus he remained in this unfortunately guise. Mr. Hyde died 20 years later in the cage of a traveling circus.

The day Ron Weasley disappeared in the Bermuda Triangle.

"Harry! So this is where all the things you conjured away, end up!"

Count the white spots in the picture and post the result

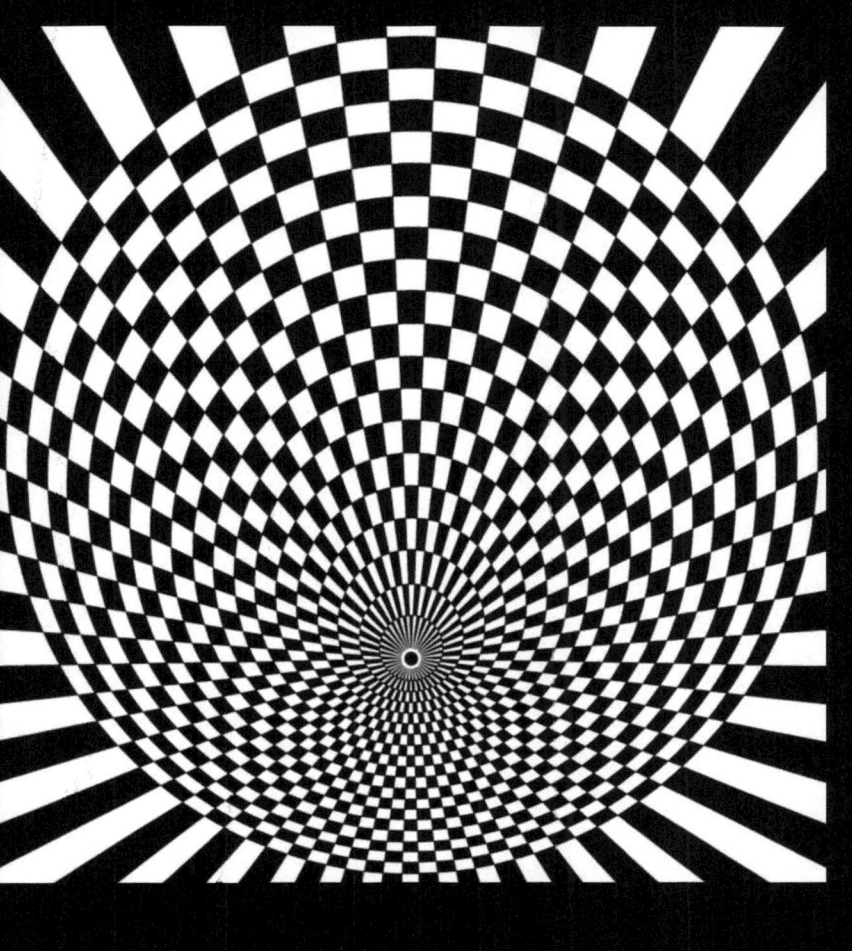

The other day at the pawnbroker

"Give me my Preeeeciousssss!!!"

"Doesn't work Gollum, Frodo was just there and exchanged it!"

The stupidest riddle in the world

Imagine you pass a cow and die.

What happened?

Solution: You fell from a slope. While flying down, you passed a ledge where a cow was standing. Then you fall further down into a raging river and die by drowning.

Digitization is also finding its way into religion

And the eleventh commandment is: You shall honor your smartphone!

What is that?

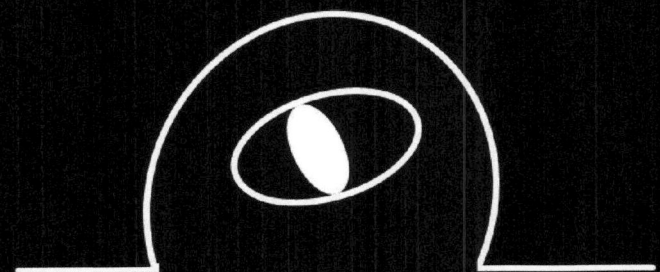

Tom looks through Jerry's mouse hole

Useless math puzzle
for your birthday

Its your birthday. One of your guests makes a bet that he can cut the birthday cake into 11 pieces with just 4 straight cuts. Is it possible?

"How would you assess our solar system?"

"A star."

Recently, at the psychiatrist

"Everyone thinks I am a horse"

How smart are you?

500 $/ € / £

Machine accepts card or bill

TESTOMAT FANTASTIC

What is that?

Baby Yoda hiding behind a box

Worlds leading microbiologist

What is this?

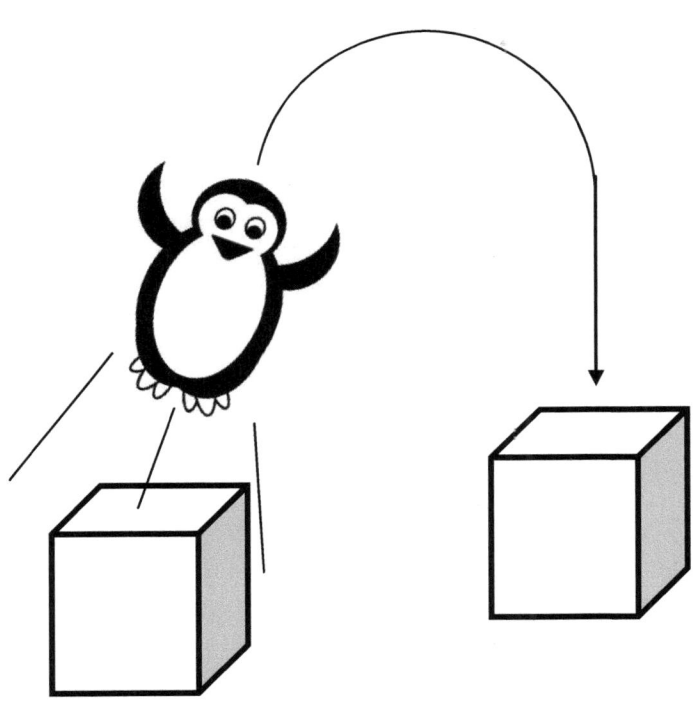

A jumpguin

The useless riddle

Andrew and Polly are proud owners of diamonds. Andrew says to Polly:

"If you give me one of your diamonds, we'll both have the same number."

Polly then replies:

"If you gave me a diamond, I would have double the number of diamonds you have."

How many diamonds do Andrew and Polly have?

The second stupidest puzzle in the world

Paul is no longer alive. He was about to eat something (cheese) when he was hit (by a piece of metal).

What had happened?

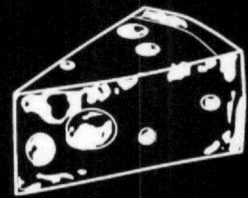

Solution: Paul is the name of a mouse. While searching for a piece of cheese, it fell victim to a mouse trap.

Oh, that's not a good sign

A particularly old photo of me

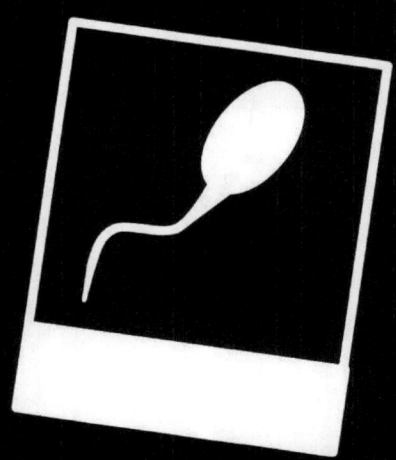

Please ignore this riddle. It's too bad.

James Bond has to escape. The bridge of salvation crosses a river of boiling hot lava. James jumps off this bridge and survive.

How is it possible?

Solution: James stood at the end of the bridge and jumped from there to the bank on the other side.

"I don't mind getting old"

"And how old are you?"

"I'm 'ntyandthree years old!"

FAQs for the Zombie Apocalypse

Question: What does the undead say when asked for directions?

Answer: Follow my finger (throws its finger).

-

Question: What does an undead do when in love?

Answer: - plucking fingers - she loves me, she loves me not...

-

Question: What do undead call skeletons?

Answer: empties.

-

Two undead meet at the graveyard at midnight. Says one:

"So you're also doing inventory?"

-

Two undead are standing on the roof of a house, one falls down, the other is also dead.

-

The last words of the doctor treating an undead: "Say Ahhhhhhh..."

A father son conversation

Caterwauling? I like. My cat in particular can play the piano very well.

Stock photo

The puzzle with an absurd solution

You have the following equation:

$$5 + 5 + 5 = 550$$

How can you get the equation right with just one stroke?

Solution: By changing the first plus sign into a four.

$$5 \, 4 \, 5 + 5 = 550$$

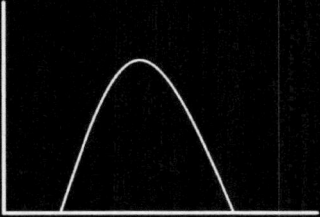

Normal distribution

Paranormal distribution

And Moses spoke:
"I have strange spots on my skin",
and the sea like this:

This is the part of the book without
content. If you still find something,
you can keep it. It's yours alone!

Treat this page with care!

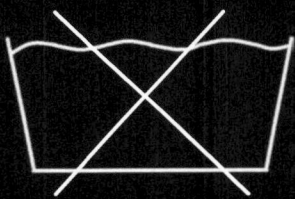

Do not wash or spin!

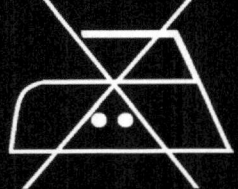

Fold and do not iron!

Reacts absorbent to fabric softener!

He really exists.
The cat Santa Claus!

Rare infrared photo

You are on an airliner, a passenger with a seat by the window.
Suddenly you hear something knocking at the window. You turn your head to the window and look into the face of a duck.
Through the window, you hear the duck say:

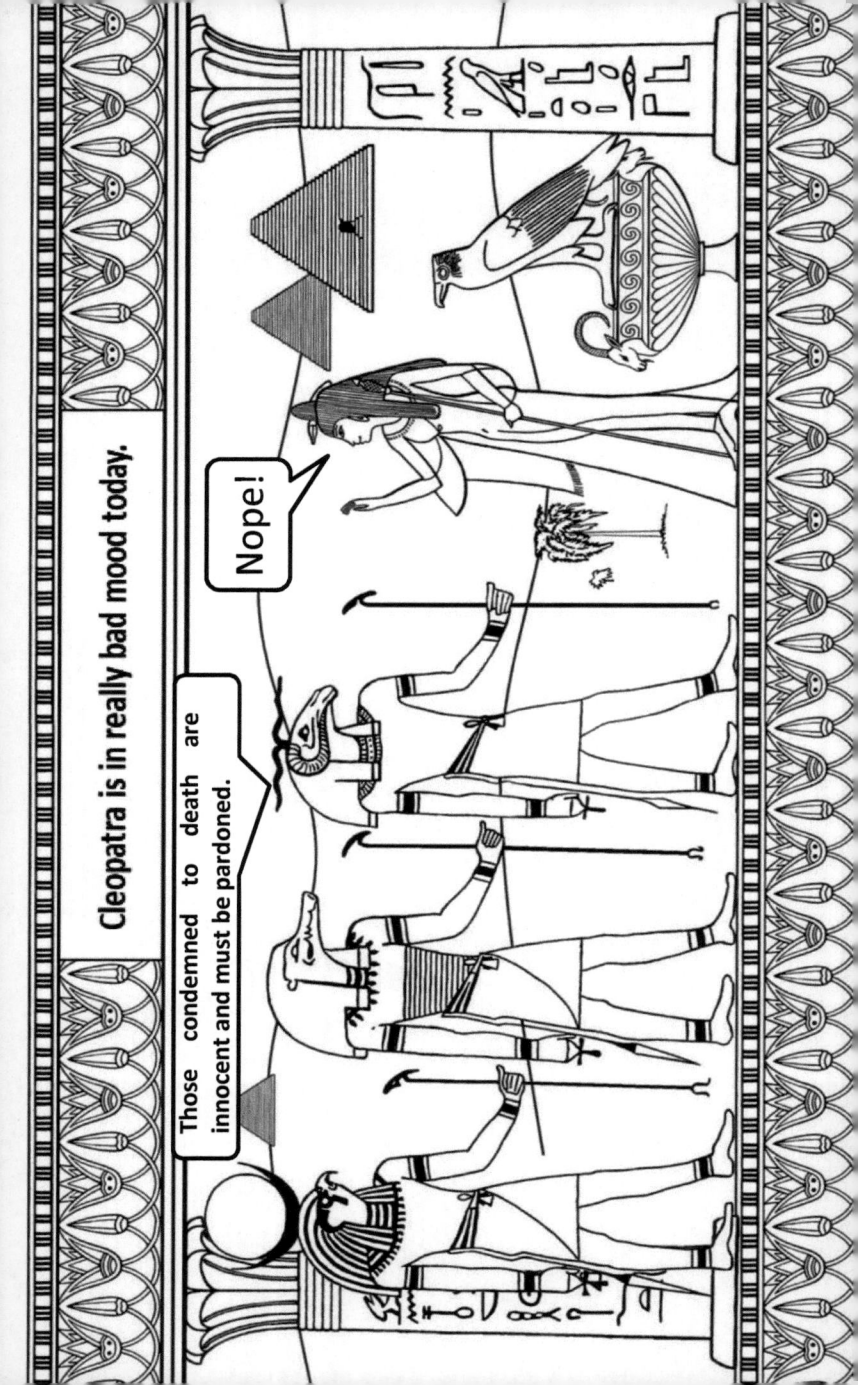

Two mexican jedis during lightsaber training

Frank can't understand why everybody thinks that hanging out is great.

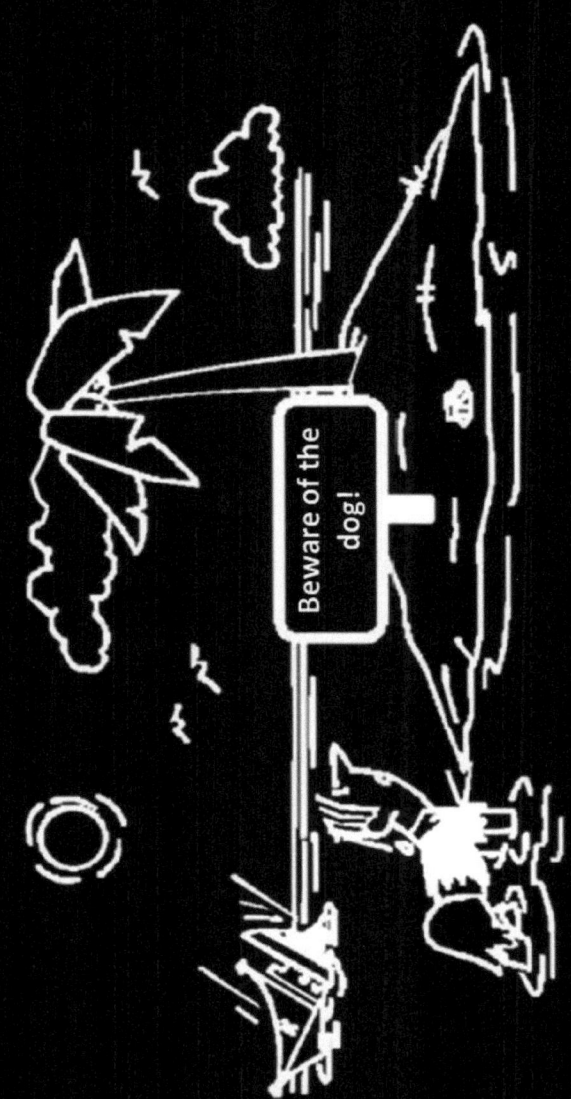

Sibling Dialogue

Everything catches fire in this book. It's packed with sharply fried short and silly jokes, as well as well cooked cartoons on the subject of barbecuing that will set the gourmet heart of every barbecue master into ecstasy. Start from the grill masters pole position into barbecue orgy of hearty humour.

Well done, gnome. This book is absolutely pointless, but funny.

Thank you, master Roogle.